P9-CBT-627

Words to Know

by HARRY BRICKER, PH.D. *and* YVONNE BECKWITH, B.F.A.

and the editors of NEW STANDARD ENCYCLOPEDIA

illustrated by DAN SICULAN

STANDARD EDUCATIONAL CORPORATION *Chicago 1985*

Harry Bricker, PH.D., is Educational Editor of *New Standard Encyclopedia.* After teaching in public schools, he served as reading specialist; information specialist; member of the Atlanta Area Teacher Education Service; and assistant professor of education at the University of Bridgeport. He is coauthor of *You Can Read Better* and *Your Child and Radio, TV, Comics, and Movies* and editor of "Sentence Structure Chart Series."

Yvonne Beckwith, B.F.A., is an editor of *New Standard Encyclopedia.* After working as a free lance illustrator she was employed as assistant art director of the Reuben H. Donnelley Corporation. She later became an editor for The Child's World, Inc. She is editor of *Countries and Their Children, The World and Its Wonders,* and *People and Great Deeds.*

Dan Siculan has illustrated numerous books and magazines for major midwestern publishers. He is especially well-known for his work in the children's field.

Standard Book Number 87392-001-5
Library of Congress Number 68-54585

Foreword

Words to Know was designed as a beginning word book for young children at various stages of reading development. Preschool children can use it on their own as a picture book, or it can be read aloud to them. As they turn the colorful pages they will find familiar people, things, and activities—stepping-stones to learning the printed letters and words. Beginning readers will recognize certain words while the picture clues will help them learn many others. More advanced readers will read complete sentences and will use the book as an aid to learning to write their own sentences and stories, particularly to look up the spelling of words.

Introducing each letter of the alphabet with one or more characters the child can identify with—Ann and Andy for A, Bob and Billy for B, Carl the clown for C, and so on—is more than just an interest-capturing device. Even the very young can soon learn that entry words in the Ann-Andy picture pages all begin with A, or that to find C words he should turn to the section on friendly Carl the clown. As he learns the A to Z order of the words he is learning a skill important for his later use of formal dictionaries.

All of the more than 1,200 different words used in this book are listed in the back along with the number of the page for each word. This alphabetic reference list is useful as an index and also as a testing-learning device; for example, it may be used to discover which words the child is able to recognize without the pictorial clues and which words he has not yet mastered.

For help in selecting the words to be included, experienced elementary school teachers in various parts of the country were consulted. A study was also made of widely used vocabulary lists and of a number of standardized tests of primary vocabulary and reading.

The Authors

A

Ann and Andy

able

Andy is able to roller skate.

about

Ann reads a book about cats.

above

Andy's balloon is above the house.

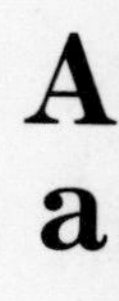

A a

across

The dog runs across the street.

add

Ann can add three and one.
"Three and one make four," she says.

address

This is Ann's address.
It tells where she lives.

afraid

Annabella is afraid of the dog.

after

The dog is running after
the cat.

afternoon

In the morning Ann plays.
In the afternoon she takes a nap.

again

Here is Andy again.
Now he is on ice skates.

against

Andy throws a ball against
the wall.

age

Andy is seven years old.
What is your age?

ahead

Annabella is walking ahead of Ann.
Ann is behind Annabella.

air

Ann blows air into a balloon.
Andy's kite is up in the air.

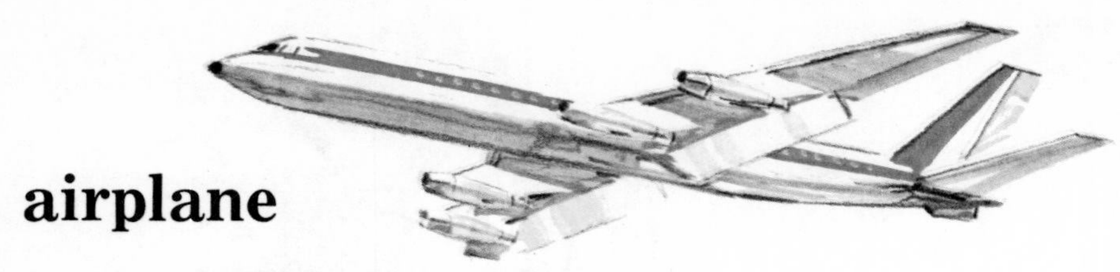

airplane

Airplanes fly in the air.
This airplane is a jet.

airport

See the planes at the airport.
This airport is a busy place.

alike

These twins look alike.
They dress alike too.

all

All the children look happy.
They are all smiling or laughing.

almost

"I'm almost as tall as you, Andy."

alone

Ann is alone.
She is playing by herself.

along

Annabella walks along the branch.

alphabet

The alphabet has 26 letters.
How many can you name?

among

Can you find an orange among the apples?

angry

Ann is angry with Annabella.
"You are a bad cat!" she says.

another

Andy took one cookie.
Now he is taking another one.

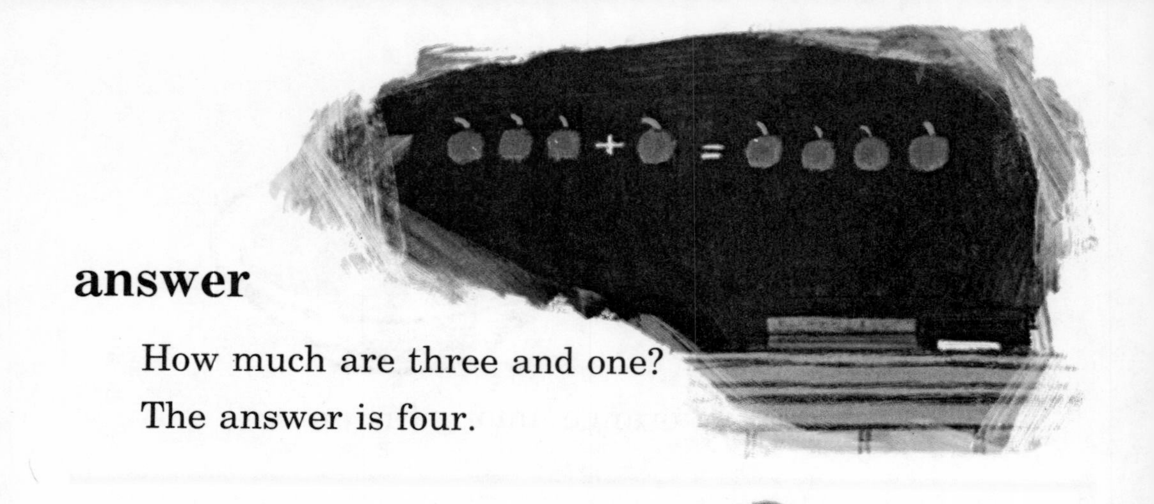

answer

How much are three and one?
The answer is four.

apron

Ann is wearing a pretty apron.

around

Around and around and around
they go.

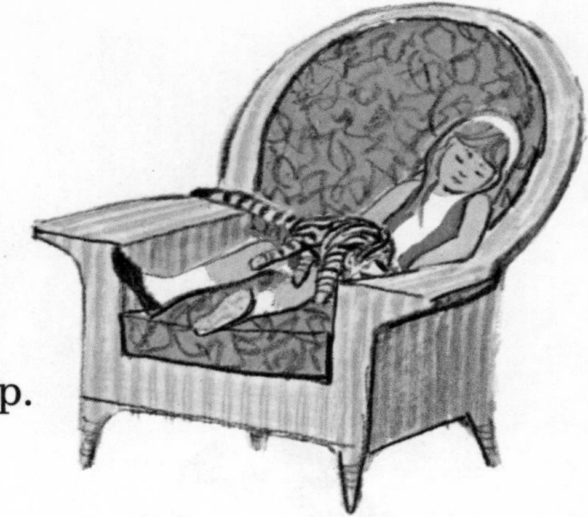

asleep

Annabella is fast asleep.
So is Ann.

automobile

Car is a short word for automobile.
Andy plays with his toy automobiles.

awake

Ann is awake.
Annabella is still sleeping.

away

Ann and Andy are going away now.
They wave good-by.

B

Bob and Billy

baby

Billy is a baby boy.

back

Billy is riding on Bob's back.

bag

Who is in the bag?
Blackie is in the bag!

ball

Billy bounces the ball to Blackie.

balloon

Bob blows up a balloon for Billy.

band

Listen to the music of the band.
Boom! Boom! goes the drum.

bank

"I save money in my piggy bank."

bark

"Bow-wow," barks Blackie.

basket

Who is hiding in the basket?

bat

Bob hit the baseball with his bat.

bath

Bob is giving Blackie a bath.

beautiful

"What a beautiful butterfly!"

bedroom

This is Bob's bedroom.

begin

The boys are ready to begin a race.

behind

Who is hiding behind the bush?

bell

"I can hear the bell ringing."

below

Billy is one step below the teddy bear.

beside

Billy is sitting beside the teddy bear.

best

"Which toy do you like best?" asks Bob.

between

Blackie ran between Bob's legs.

bib

Billy is wearing a bib.

bicycle

Bike is a short word for bicycle.
Bob is riding his bicycle.

big

Blackie is a small dog.
The other dog is big.

bird

Bob put some bread out for the birds.

birthday

Today is Bob's birthday.
Can you tell how old he is?

bite

Bob takes a big bite
of his cake.

blackboard

Read the word on the blackboard.

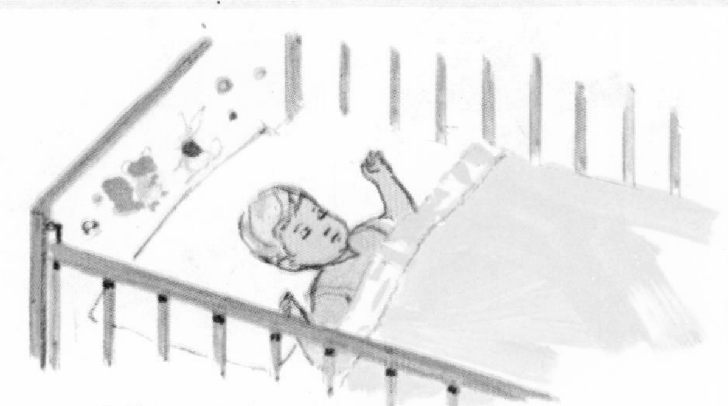

blanket

Billy's blanket keeps him warm.

block

What letter is on the block?

boat

One boat is a sailboat.
The other is a motorboat.

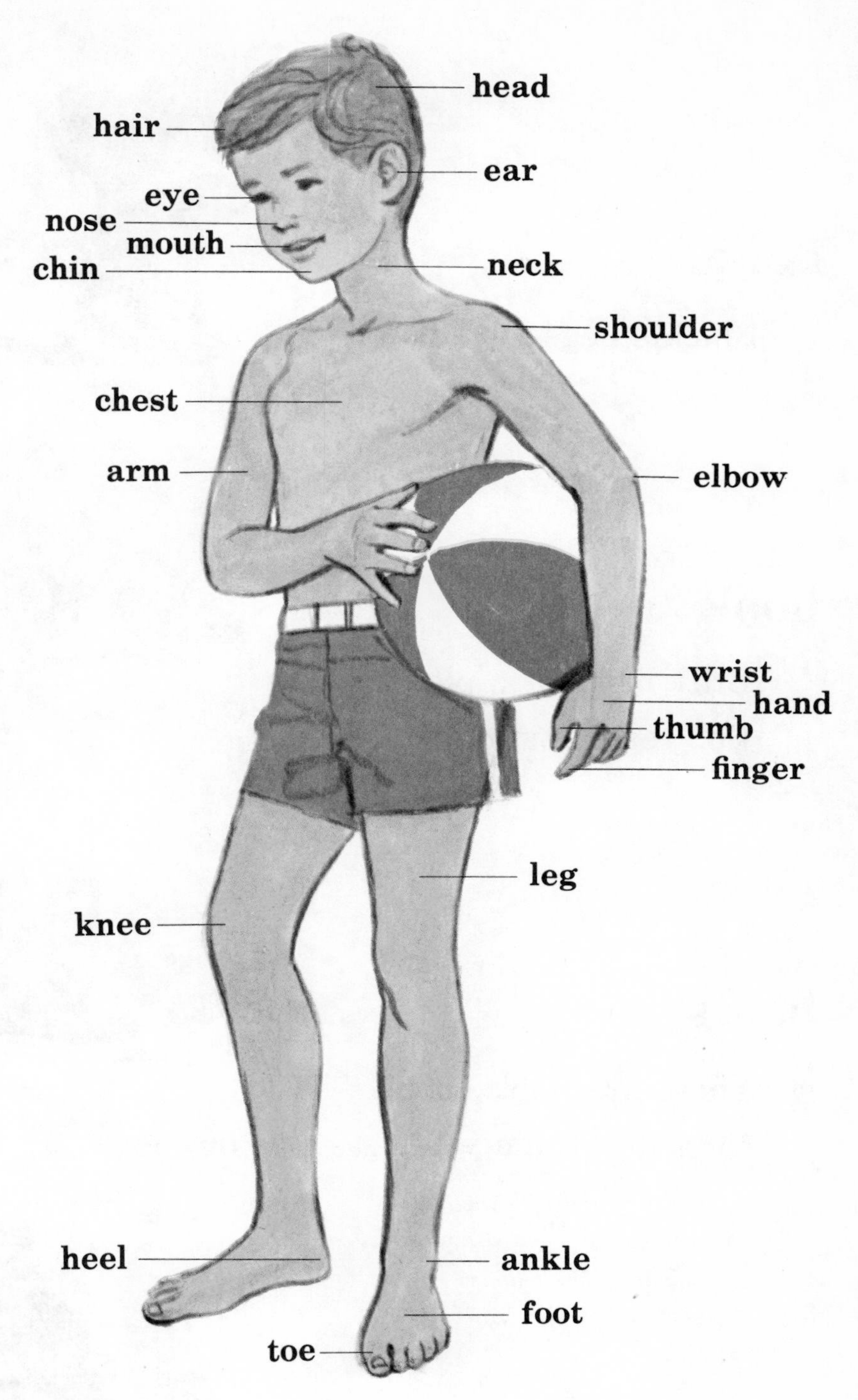

body

Name as many parts of the body as you can.

bone

Blackie begs for a bone.

book

Billy looks at a picture book.
Bob reads a storybook.

boots

These are Bob's boots.
He wears them when it rains or snows.

both

Are both boys asleep?

bottle

Billy drinks milk from his bottle.

bottom

Which block is on the bottom?
Which one is on the top?

bow

Bob tied his shoelace in a bow.
Can you tie a bow?

box

Bob puts Billy's toys in a box.

boy

The boys are playing football.
One boy carries the ball.

branch

Bob swings from the branch of a tree.

break

Did Billy's bowl break?
Yes, it broke in two.

breakfast

In the morning Bob eats breakfast.

bridge

Bob is standing on a bridge.

What is going under the bridge?

bring

"Bring me the stick, Blackie."

broom

Bob sweeps the porch with a broom.

brother

Bob and Billy are brothers.

bubble

Billy is trying to catch a bubble.

build

Bob builds a birdhouse.

bump

Did Billy bump his head?

burn

"Be careful, Billy. Don't burn yourself!"

bus

Bob gets on the bus.
The bus takes him to school.

butter

Bob likes butter on toast.

button

Billy lost a button from his coat.

Carl the Clown

call

"Help, help," Carl calls.
"I'm stuck!"

camera

Carl takes a picture with his camera.

can

"I can do a cartwheel," says Carl.
"Can you?"

canary

A canary is a bird.
Carl has a pet canary.

candle

Carl lit a candle.

catch

Catch those boxes, Carl!
Catch them before they fall.

chair

The dog is in the chair.
The chair is in the air.

chase

Look at the clowns chase each other.

children

The children like Carl.
He likes the children.

chocolate

Carl gave chocolate clowns
to the children.

circle

The children made a circle.
Carl is inside the circle.

circus

A circus is a big show.
Carl is a circus clown.

city

Carl is in the city.

He looks at the tall buildings.

clap

The children clap their hands.

clean

One glove is clean.

The other one is dirty.

climb

Carl climbs up the ladder.

clock

Carl looks at the clock.
"It's three o'clock," he says.

close

Close the door of the cage, Carl!

clothes

These are Carl's circus clothes.

coat

Carl is wearing a long coat.

cold

"It's cold outside. Brrr," says Carl.

colors

Carl painted these colors.
Can you name all eleven?

comb

Carl combs his hair with a big comb.

come

"Come in," says Carl.

"I'm glad you came."

corner

Carl rides around the corner.

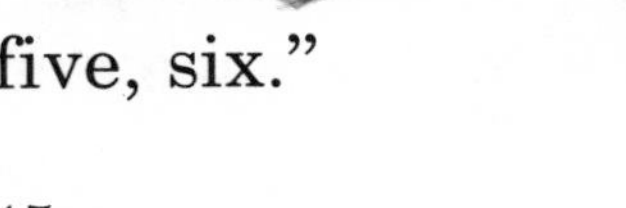

count

Carl counts six hats.

"One, two, three, four, five, six."

country

Carl is in the country.
He looks at the farms.

---

cover

Carl covers his eyes.
"Peek-a-boo," he says.

---

crayon

Carl is coloring with crayons.

crowd

See the crowd of people.
Carl waves to the crowd.

cry

"Please don't cry," says Carl.
"Maybe I can make you laugh."

cut

What did Carl cut out?

D

Daddy and Donna

dance

Donna dances to the music.

dark

Donna has dark hair.
Daddy has light hair.

days

"These are the days of the week,"
says the teacher. "Can you name them?"

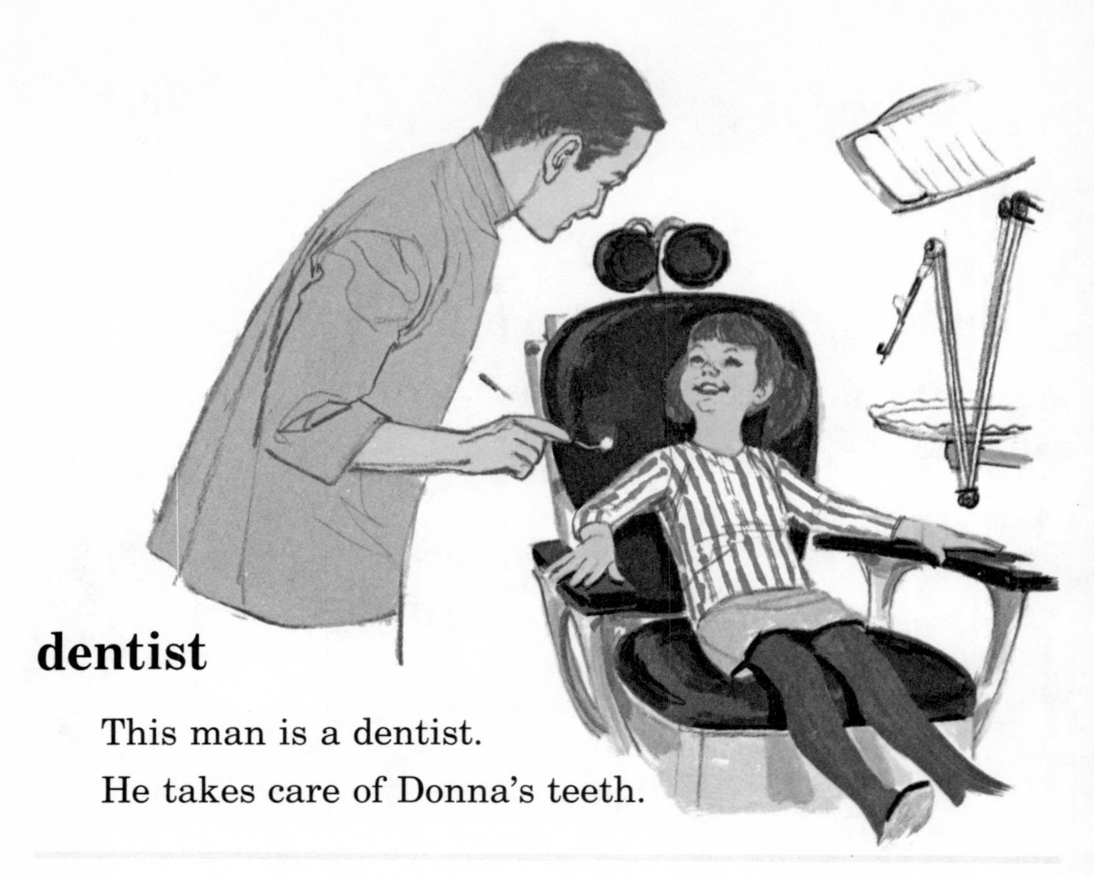

dentist

This man is a dentist.
He takes care of Donna's teeth.

desk

The teacher sits at her desk.
The children sit at their desks.

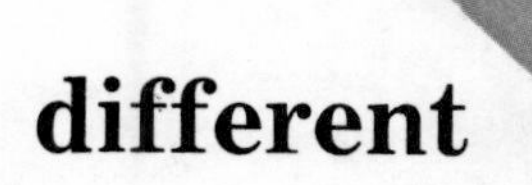

different

"Three are the same.
Which one is different?"

dig

Donna digs in the sand.

dinner

"Oh, goody!" says Donna.
"We're having turkey for dinner."

dirt

Donna has dirt on her hands.
Her face is dirty too.

doctor

Donna is sick today.
"You will soon be well," says the doctor.

doll

Donna plays with her dolls.

door

Daddy opens the door for Mother.

down

There goes Donna down the slide.

dozen

"Mother bought a dozen eggs.
A dozen is twelve," says Donna.

draw

What did Daddy draw?

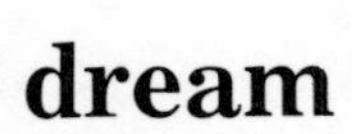

dream

Donna is dreaming.

Is it a good dream?

dress

Donna buttons her dress.

"I can dress myself," she says.

drink

Daddy pours a glass of milk.

Donna will drink it.

drive

Daddy drives his car to work.

drop

"Carry these carefully.
Don't drop them."

dry

Mother washed Donna's hair.
Donna uses a towel to dry it.

E

Ed

early

It is early in the morning.
Ed gets up early.

easy

Ed can touch his toes.
"This is easy," he says.

eat

Ed eats cereal for breakfast.

edge

Ed is sitting on the edge of his chair.

empty

The glass is full of milk.
The pitcher is empty.

end

Ed pulls one end of the rope.
The puppy pulls the other end.

engine

"The engine makes the car go," says Ed.

enjoy

Ed likes puppet shows.
"I enjoy them," he says.

enough

"This is not big enough.
It's too small for me."

ever

"Have you ever done this?"

every

"I fed every puppy," says Ed.
"They were all hungry."

everything

The puppies ate everything
in their bowls. Nothing is left.

F

Fred and His Family

face

Fred made a funny face.

family

Here are Father, Mother, Fred, and Fran.
There are four people in this family.

farm

Fred's family lives on a farm.

F
f

farmer

Father works on his farm.
He is a farmer.

fast

Fred likes to ride fast.

fasten

"Fasten your seat belt, Fran."

fat

Look at the fat little pigs.

father

Father has two children.

Fred is his son. Fran is his daughter.

feed

Fred feeds the chickens.

feel

"Feel how soft its fur is."

fell

Fred fell off his pony.

"I didn't get hurt," he says.

fence

The fence is broken.

Father is mending it.

fight

There is a fight on television.

Father and Fred watch the fight.

fill

"Fill the pail, Fred.
I want a full pail."

fire

Father puts a log
on the fire.

first

"Wash your hands first," says Mother.
"Then you may eat."

fish

Fish live in water.

Fred caught a fish with a worm.

fit

"These shoes don't fit me.
They are the wrong size."

fix

"Help me fix my flashlight, Dad."

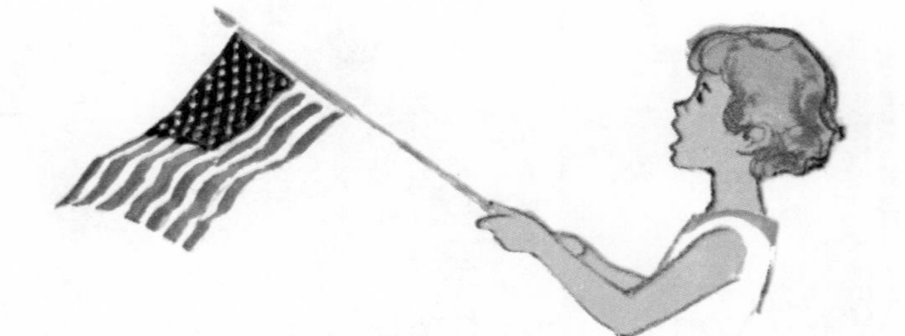

flag

The American flag is red, white, and blue.

flat

Fred's bike has a flat tire.
"I can fix it," he says.

float

Fred can float.
Can you?

floor

Fred and Fran are playing on the floor.

flower

The bee goes from flower to flower.

fly

"Don't fly away," says Fran.

food

Food is kept cold
in the refrigerator.

forget

What did Fred forget to do?

found

Fran found her other shoe.

fourth

"One, two, three, four," says Fran.
"I am fourth in line."

fresh

Fred is selling fresh corn.
He picked it this morning.

friend

Fred and his friend Joe
are riding ponies.

frighten

The ponies frighten the chickens.
See them run!

front

The car is in front of the house.
The truck is in the back.

fruit

Read the name of each fruit.
Which fruit do you like best?

fun

"This is fun!" says Fred.
"We're having a great time!"

G

Grandpa, Grandma, and Gay

game

Games are fun to play.
Three can play this game.

garden

Grandpa has a garden.
What is growing in his garden?

gate

Gay opens
the gate to the garden.

get

What did Gay get? She got a present.

gift

"Thank you for the gift," says Gay.

girl

"I got a girl doll and a boy doll."

give

Gay gives Grandpa a kiss.

glad

"We're glad you like your gift."

glass

The window is made of glass.

glasses

Gay's glasses help her see better.

gloves

Grandpa wears gloves
when he works in the garden.

gold

Grandma's ring is made of gold.

good-by

"Good-by, Grandpa. I'm going to school now."

grade

Gay is in the second grade.
Last year she was in first grade.

grandfather
grandmother

Grandpa is Gay's grandfather.
Grandma is Gay's grandmother.

grass

Grandpa cuts the grass.

ground

Gay is planting flower seeds
in the ground.

grow

Rain helps the flowers grow.

guess

"Guess who," says Gay.

gum

Gay likes bubble gum.

H

Henry and Harvey

half

Henry gives one half to Harvey.
He keeps the other half for himself.

hall

Henry walks down the hall at school.

Halloween

The boys dress up on Halloween.
"Trick or treat," they say.

hammer

Henry hits a nail with a hammer.

handkerchief

"Achoo!" Harvey uses his handkerchief when he sneezes.

hang

"Hang your jacket on a hanger," says Mother.

happen

"How did it happen, Henry?"

"I went so fast the wheel came off."

happy

Harvey is happy because he hit a home run.

hate

"I hate peas," says Henry.
"I like them," says Harvey.

hear

"I can hear Hildegarde purr."

heart

Henry drew a heart.

heavy

"This box is heavy,"
says Harvey. "I can't lift it."

---

hello

"Hello, Henry? This is Harvey."

help

"Don't worry, Hildegarde.
I'll help you get down."

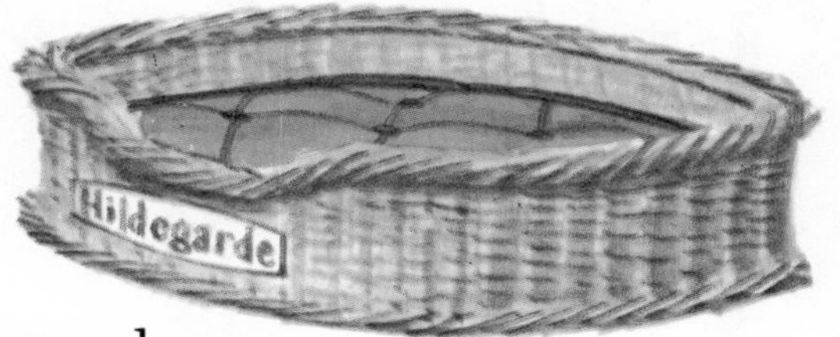

here

Hildegarde sleeps here.

hide

Henry and Harvey play hide and seek.

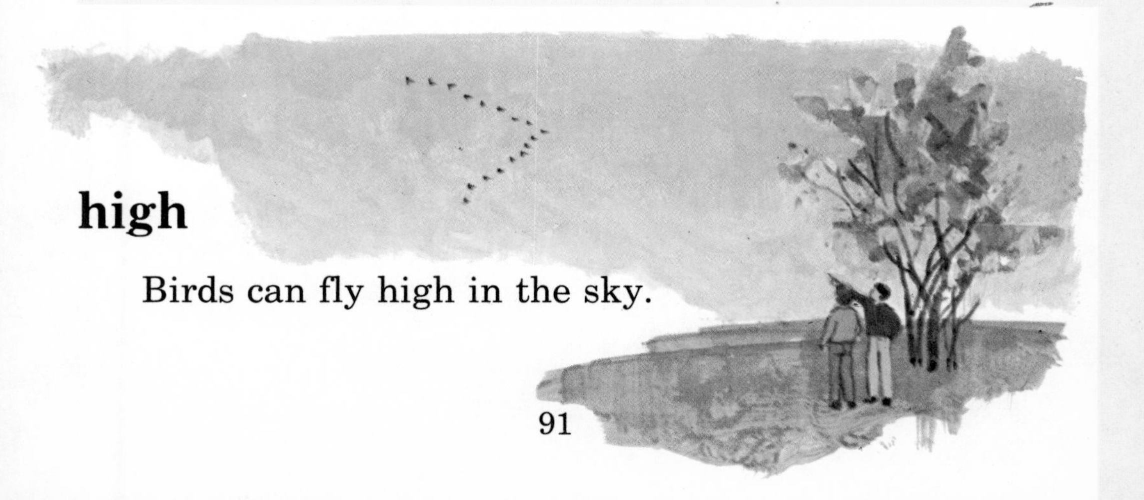

high

Birds can fly high in the sky.

hill

The boys pull their sleds up the hill.

his

Hildegarde belongs to Henry.
She is his cat.

hit

"Ouch, I hit my finger."

hold

Henry holds the box.
The box holds Hildegarde.

hole

Henry has a hole in his pocket.

home

"Is Henry home?"
asks Harvey.

hop

Henry hops on one foot.

horn

Harvey blows his horn.

hot

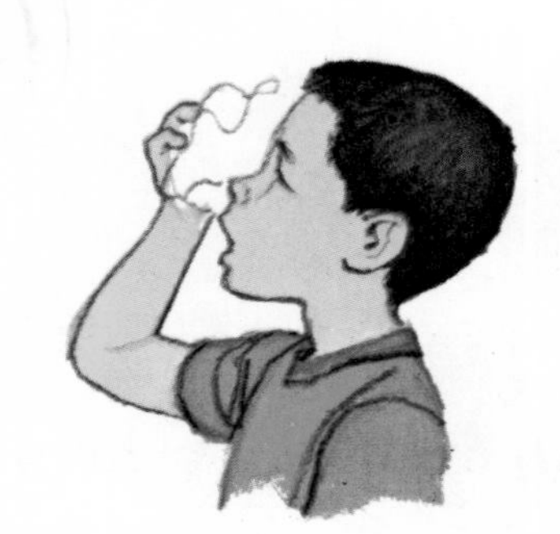

It's a very warm day.
"I'm hot," says Harvey.

house

Harvey lives in this house.

hungry

"Mew, mew."
Hildegarde must be hungry.

hunt

Henry hunts for his books.

hurry

"Hurry, Henry,
or you'll miss the bus."

hurt

"Does it still hurt?" asks Harvey.
"Not anymore," answers Henry.

I

Ida and Ira

ice

Ice is cold.

Ida puts ice in her lemonade.

ice cream

Ida has a dish of ice cream.

Ira has an ice cream cone.

Indian

Ida and Ira are Indian children.

They go to an Indian school.

inside

The children are inside the school.
What is outside?

invite

"I want to invite you to my party.
Come tomorrow after school."

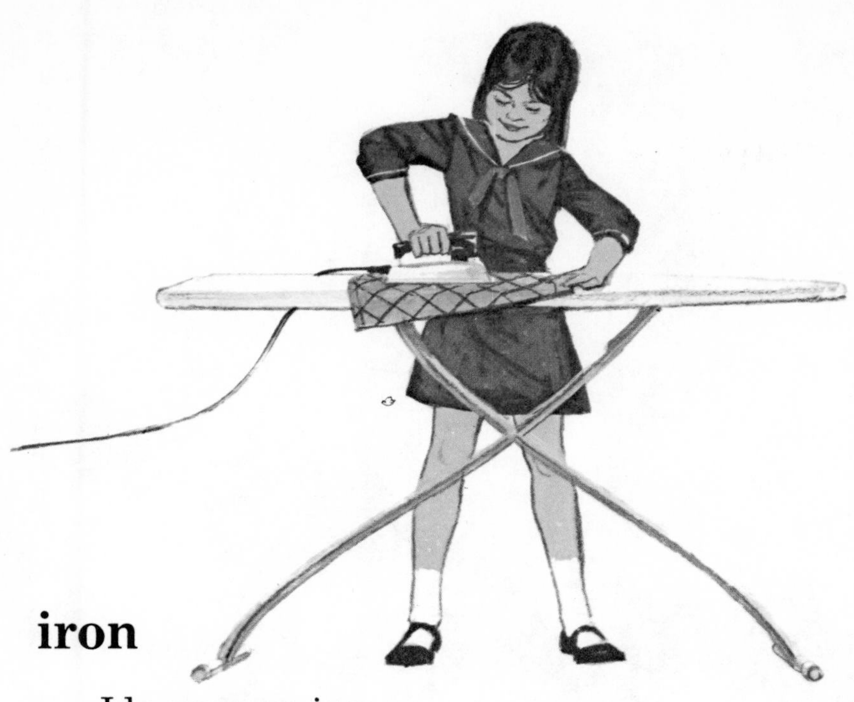

iron

Ida uses an iron.
She irons her skirt.

island

Ida and Ira are rowing
around an island.

J

Jeff

jacket

Jeff's jacket is made of wool.

jar

"I know what's in that jar.
Do you?"

joke

"What a good joke!
That's really funny!"

jump

"Watch me jump over this fence."

Kathy

keep

Kathy keeps her pennies in this bank.

key

Kathy opens her bank with a key.

kick

"Kick the ball to me," yells Ken.

kind

"Always be kind to animals.
Don't hurt them," says Kathy.

kindergarten

In kindergarten children learn and play.

kiss

Kathy gives her little brother a hug and a kiss.

kitchen

Mother cooks and bakes in the kitchen.

knife

Mother peels potatoes with a sharp knife.

knit

Mother is teaching Kathy to knit.

knock

Ken knocks on the door.
Kathy hears his knock.

know

Kathy and Ken know how to read.
Does Kathy's little brother know how?

Linda and Lucky

ladder

Linda is on a ladder.
It helps her reach up high.

lamp

Linda's lamp has a pretty shade.

land

Linda is in the water.
Lucky is on land.

large

The large dog
is next to the small dog.

last

The small dog is last.

late

School has started and
Linda is late.

laugh

Lucky is chasing his tail.
He makes Linda laugh.

lazy

"Lazy Linda, will you get up,
will you get up, will you get up?"

leaf

A leaf fell on Linda's head.
She is raking leaves.

learn

Children learn many things in school.
They learn to read and write.

left

Linda's left shoe is in her right hand.

let

"Please let me hold the baby."

letter

Linda is reading a letter.
The letter begins, "Dear Linda."

lick

Linda licks a lollipop.

light

Look at the light before you cross.

lightning

"How bright the lightning is."

like

Linda looks like her mother.

line

Linda draws a straight line.

listen

" I like to listen to the rain."

live

Linda lives in the big house.
Where does Lucky live?

long

Linda put on a long stocking.

lost

Her other stocking is lost.
"I can't find it anywhere," she says.

loud

"Turn the television down, please.
It's much too loud."

love

Linda loves her mother and father.
"We love each other," she says.

low

Lucky lies on a low step.
Linda sits on a higher step.

lunch

Linda has a sandwich for lunch.

M

Mother and Mary Ann

mail

The postman brings the mail.
"Thank you," says Mother.

make

Mary Ann helps Mother
make cupcakes.

many

How many cupcakes did they make?

marbles

The boys are playing marbles.

march

Look at the boys march.
They are marching in a parade.

may

"Mother, may I go out to play?"

meal

Mother is getting a meal ready.

meat

"We are having meat for supper,"
says Mary Ann.

meet

Father is home from work.
Mother meets him at the door.

middle

The children are standing in a circle.
Who is in the middle?

mile

"How far is it to Madison?" asks Mary Ann.
"It is one mile," says Father.

minute

"There are sixty seconds in one minute," says Mother.

miss

"I must hurry or I'll miss my bus," says Father.

mittens

Mary Ann had two mittens but she lost one.

money

Mary Ann is learning the names for money.

JANUARY FEBRUARY
MARCH APRIL MAY
JUNE JULY AUGUST
SEPTEMBER OCTOBER
NOVEMBER DECEMBER

months

"There are twelve months in a year."

moon

"Look at the moon, Mother.
Isn't it round and bright?"

more

"Could I have some more cake?"

most

Mary Ann ate most of her cake.
She left a little.

mother

"I am pretending I'm a mother,"
says Mary Ann.

movie

Father and Mother and Mary Ann
are watching a movie.

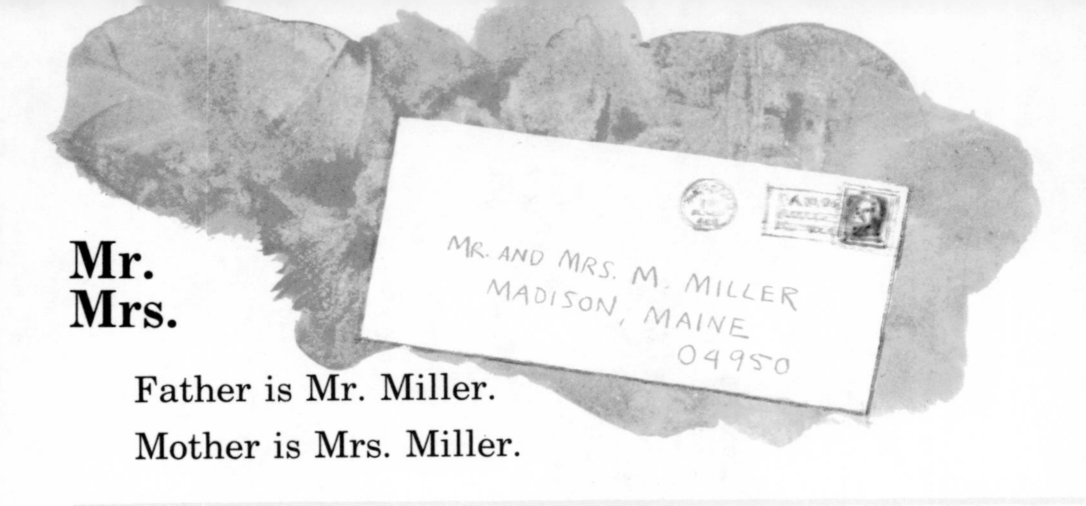

Mr.
Mrs.

Father is Mr. Miller.

Mother is Mrs. Miller.

much

"Does it hurt much?" asked Mother.

"No, just a little bit."

mud

Mary Ann is making mud pies.

N

Nancy and Norma

nail

Nancy hangs a picture on a nail.

---

name

"My name is Nancy.
My friend's name is Norma."

nearly

The glass is nearly full.
The pitcher is nearly empty.

need

Norma has one nickel.
"But I need another one," she says.

needle

Nancy is sewing with a needle and thread.

neighbor

Norma lives next door to Nancy.
She is Nancy's neighbor.

nest

The girls found a robin's nest.
There are eggs in the nest.

never

"Never leave toys on the steps, Nancy.
That's no place for them."

new

"Do you like my new dress?"

newspaper

The dog brought Nancy
the newspaper.

night

After day comes night.
It is dark at night.

no

"No, no," says Nancy. "Don't do that."

noise

The rattle makes a noise.
The baby likes the noise.

nothing

"My purse is empty," says Nancy.
"There is nothing in it."

1 ONE
2 TWO
3 THREE
4 FOUR
5 FIVE
6 SIX
7 SEVEN
8 EIGHT
9 NINE
10 TEN
11 ELEVEN
12 TWELVE

numbers

Here are two ways to show numbers.

nurse

This woman is a nurse.
Nancy wants to be a nurse someday.

O

Owen

off

The wind blew Owen's cap off.

often

Owen plays baseball often.
He plays almost every day.

oil

"The wheels turn better
after I oil them."

old

Owen likes to listen
to the old man's stories.

once

"I'll try once more,"
says Owen.

only

Owen has two sisters
but only one brother.

other

One wagon is red.

What color is the other one?

outside

The children are outside.

They like to play outdoors.

own

This wagon belongs to Owen.

"I own it," he says.

Pam and Penny

package

"This package is for you, Penny.
The mailman brought it."

page

"Aunt Martha sent me a book.
There's a picture on every page."

paint

Pam likes to paint.
She is painting Penny's picture.

pair

"These shoes match," says Penny.
"They make a pair."

pajamas

Penny put on her pajamas.
Now she is ready for bed.

pan

Pam is frying eggs in a pan.

paper

Penny is playing
with her paper dolls.

parade

"Here comes the parade!
Look who's in front!"

park

Penny is feeding pigeons in the park.

part

"My puppy is part brown and part white."

party

Everyone is having fun at Penny's party.

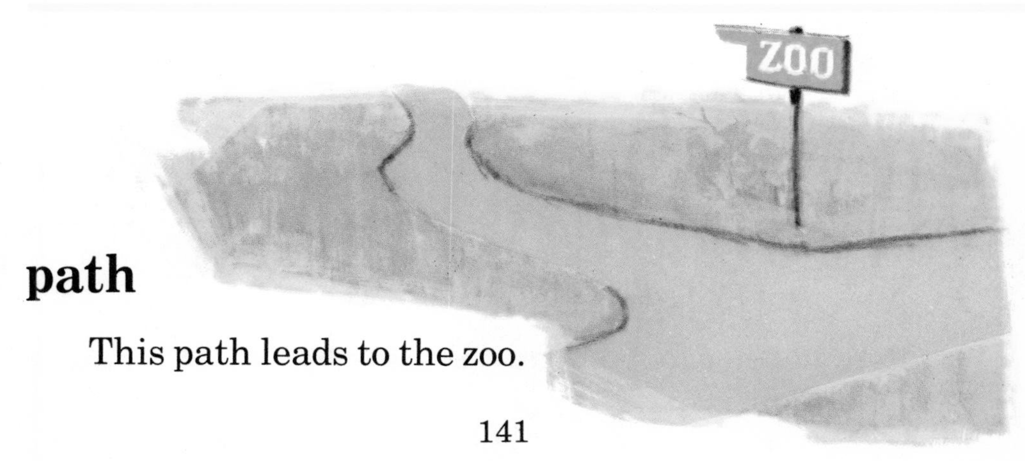

path

This path leads to the zoo.

pay

Penny bought a bag of peanuts.
How much did she pay?

peanut

Penny gave a peanut to the squirrel.

pedal

A bicycle has two pedals.
Pam has her foot on one pedal.

pen

Pam writes her name with a pen.

pencil

Penny prints her name with a pencil.

people

The girls are at a football game.
"Look at all the people," says Penny.

pepper

Pam is filling the pepper shaker.

pets

These animals are pets.

Do you have a pet?

piano

Pam is learning to play the piano.

pick

"Mother likes wild flowers.
Let's pick some for her, Penny."

picnic

The girls are having a picnic today.

picture

"Sit still," says Pam.
"I want to take your picture."

piece

"I like watermelon.
May I have a big piece?"

pin

Pam has a pretty pin.
She wears it on her dress.

plant

Every plant needs water.

play

Pam is in a school play.
She is the princess in the play.

playground

Penny and her friends are playing on the playground.

pot

Penny needs a new pot for her plant.

pour

"I'll pour some tea for you," says Penny to her doll.

present

Penny gave Pam a birthday present.

pretty

"What a pretty package!" says Pam.
"Did you wrap it yourself?"

pull

"Hurry, Pam, pull the ribbon off
and open it."

purse

"Thank you for the purse," says Pam.
"I needed a new one."

Queenie

quart

This is a quart of milk.

quick

Queenie is quick.

quiet

Sometimes Queenie is as quiet as a mouse.

quite

Sometimes Queenie is quite loud.

R

Ricardo and Rita

race

Ricardo and Rita are in a race.
"I can beat you," says Ricardo.

radio

Rita is listening to her radio.

rain

"I hope the rain stops so we can
go out and play," says Ricardo.

rainbow

"Look at the beautiful rainbow!"

ranch

The children live on a cattle ranch.
Their father is a rancher.

read

Ricardo likes to read stories about cowboys and horses.

ready

"Let's race again," says Rita. "Ready, set, go!"

remember

"Remember to feed your horse," says Father. "Don't forget."

rest

Father is tired. He is taking a rest.

ribbon

Rita tied her hair with a ribbon.

ride

Ricardo and Rita like to ride horseback.

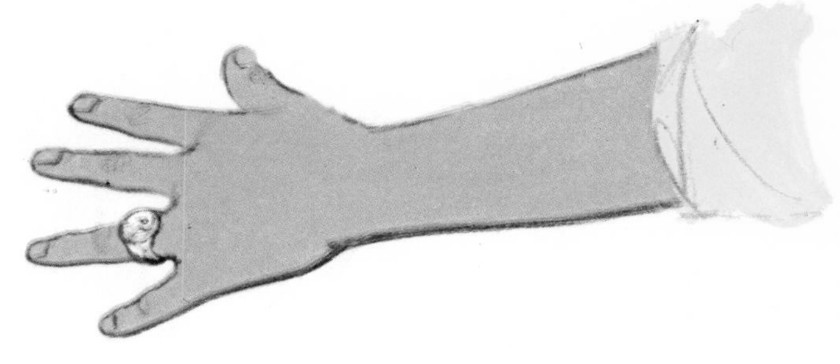

ring

Rita wears a silver ring on her finger.

road

Ricardo and Rita are walking
by the side of the road.

rock

The children are climbing on a big rock.

roll

"Roll over," says Rita.

roof

Rita's doll house has a red roof.

room

"My doll house has a living room,
bedroom, kitchen, and bathroom."

root

"Look at the long root
on this weed," says Ricardo.

rope

Ricardo is learning to throw a rope.

row

"I see seven blackbirds,
all in a row."

rub

"There's something in my eye."
"Don't rub it," says Father.

rubbers

Rita is putting on her rubbers.
They fit over her shoes.

run

"I can run faster than you,"
says Ricardo.

S

Sam, Sue, and Miss Smith

safe

"Look both ways," says Miss Smith,
"and you will be safe."

sail

Sam is sailing his boat. It has a red sail.

salt

Sue puts some salt in her soup.

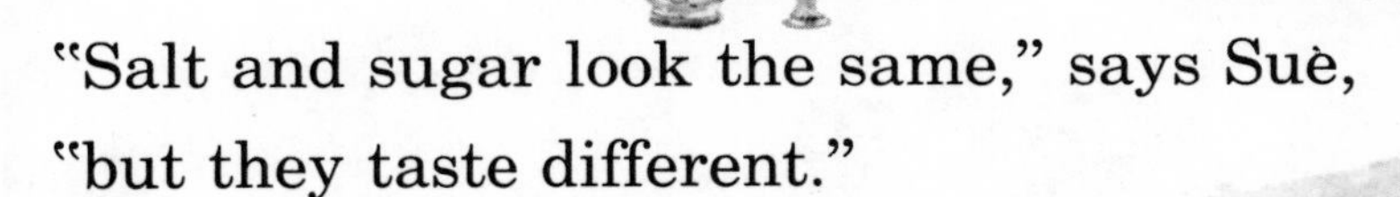

same

"Salt and sugar look the same," says Sue, "but they taste different."

sand

Sue is covering Sam's feet with sand.

Santa Claus

Sam took Sue to see Santa Claus.
"Have you been a good girl?" asks Santa.

saw

Sam uses a saw to cut a board.

school

Sam and Sue go to school.
Miss Smith teaches school.

scissors

Sue cuts paper with her scissors.

spring

summer

seasons

There are four seasons in a year.

fall

winter

second

Sue is first in line.
Sam is second.

secret

Sue tells Sam a secret.
"Don't tell anyone, Sam."

seed

Sam is planting seeds.
What kind is he planting?

sell

Sam and Sue sell lemonade.
Miss Smith buys some.

send

"Please send Sue home.
It is time for her dinner."

I am Miss Smith

sentence

Miss Smith wrote a sentence.
Can you read it?

set

Sue set the table.

Name as many things on the table as you can.

sew

Miss Smith likes to sew.

She is sewing a dress.

shade

Sniffy is sleeping in the shade
because it is cool there.

shadow

"I can make a shadow
that looks like a rabbit," says Sue.

shake

"Shake hands, Sniffy,"
says Sam. "Give me your paw."

shell

Sue found a pretty shell.
She found it at the shore.

shine

"Shine your shoes before you go
to school," says Mother.

ship

Sam is watching the ship
go down the river.

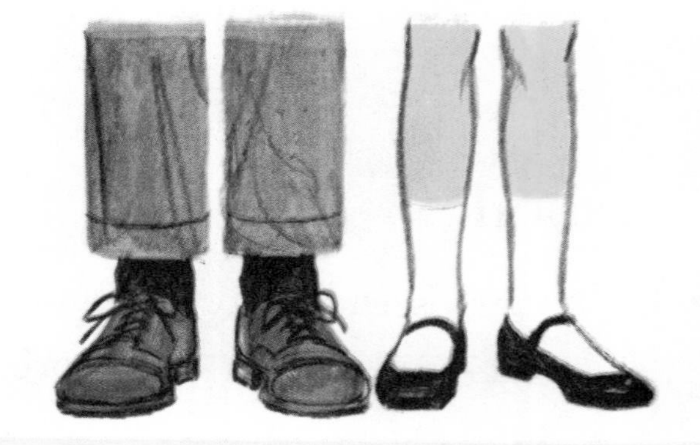

shoes

Point to Sam's shoes.
Point to Sue's shoes.

shop

Sue is helping Mother shop.
She says, "Buy this, Mama."

shore

Sam is in the water.
Sue is on the shore.

short

"My skirt is short," says Sue.
"It is shorter than yours."

shout

Sam shouts,
"Here, Sniffy, here, Sniffy."

show

"Show me your frog, Sam.
Let me see it."

shut

Sam shut one window.
"Shall I close the other one, too?"

side

Sam is on one side.
Sue is on the other side.

sign

Sam is reading the sign.
Can you read it?

sing

The children like to sing
"Three Blind Mice."

sister

Sue is Sam's little sister.

sit

"Sit up, Sniffy," says Sam.

size

This hat is the wrong size.
Sam needs a smaller size.

sky

The sky is blue.
Clouds are in the sky.

sled

Sniffy is riding on Sam's sled.

sleep

Sue went to sleep.
Sam is sleepy too.

slide

"It's fun to slide
on the ice," says Sue.

slip

"Be careful. Don't slip," says Sam.

slipper

Sniffy is carrying Sue's slipper.

slow

"A turtle is a slow animal," says Sue.

---

small

Sniffy is a small dog,
but the other dog is smaller.

---

smell

Miss Smith is smelling a rose.
"Roses smell sweet," she says.

smile

Point to the smile.
Then point to the frown.

snap

Sue can snap her fingers. Can you?

snow

Snow is white and cold.
Sam and Sue are making a snowman.

soap

Sue washes her hands with soap.

socks

Sue is wearing pink socks.
Do they match her dress?

soft

Sniffy won't sleep on the hard floor.
He likes the soft rug.

some

Sam has some candy.
Does Sue have any?

something

"There is something in the box.
I can hear it rattle."

sorry

"Oh, I'm sorry," says Sue.

spill

"I didn't mean to spill
it on you, Sam."

spin

Sue made the top spin
around and around.

splash

Sam and Sue splash each other.

spot

Miss Smith got an ink spot
on her dress.

stairs

Sam is going up the stairs.
Sue is going down the stairs.

star

On a clear night you can see many stars.

start

What time does school start?
Look at the clock.

stay

"Stay there," says Sam.
"Don't go away."

step

Sue takes a tiny step.
Sam takes a great big step.

stick

Sam draws a picture with a stick.

stockings

Sue is wearing red stockings.
Stockings are longer than socks.

stone

"I found a little stone
in my shoe," says Sam.

stop

Miss Smith saw the stop sign.
She stopped.

store

What kind of store is this?

story

Miss Smith is reading a story.
"Once upon a time," she reads.

stove

Sue is cooking on her toy stove.

---

straight

"My hair is straight. Yours is curly."

street

"What a busy street.
I must drive carefully."

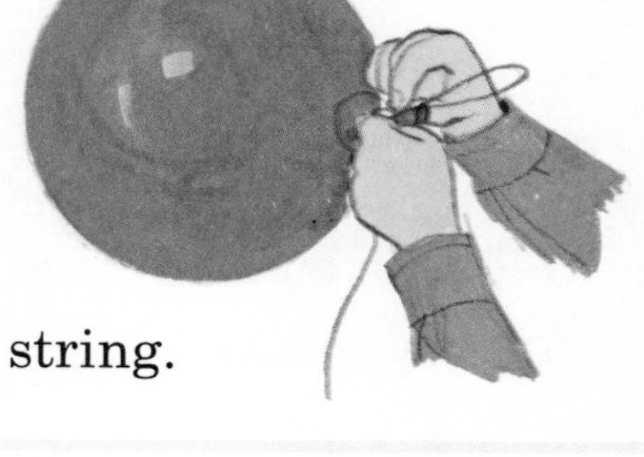

string

Sam ties the balloon with a string.

strong

"You're very strong, Sam," says Sue.

suit

Sam is wearing a brown suit.

sun

The sun is bright.

Miss Smith is wearing sunglasses.

surprise

"Did you bring me a surprise?" asks Sue.

"Yes, guess what it is," says Sam.

sweater

Sue took off her red wool sweater.

"It was too warm," she says.

sweet

"Candy is sweet," says Sue.
"Sometimes it's sour," says Sam.

swim

Sam can swim across the pool.

swing

"Push me higher," says Sue.
"It's fun to swing high."

T

Tim and Tom

T
t

table

"Please come to the table.
Supper is ready," says Mother.

tail

Tim is making a tail for his kite.

take

Mother said Tom could take a banana.

talk

"Hello? This is Tim.
May I talk to Tom?"

tall

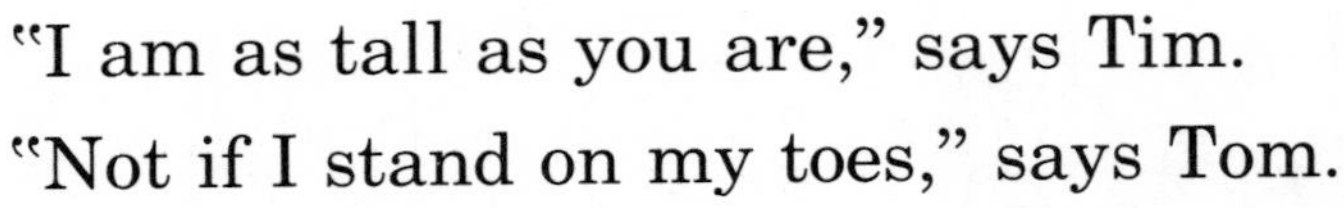

"I am as tall as you are," says Tim.
"Not if I stand on my toes," says Tom.

taste

"Potato chips taste salty," says Tim.

tear

"How did you tear your kite?" asked Father.
"I tore it on a tree branch," said Tim.

television

The boys are watching television.
"We like TV."

tell

"Tell us another story, Dad.
You tell such funny ones!"

tent

It's fun to make a tent. Tim and Tom
made theirs out of blankets.

thick

"I have a thick book.
Yours is a thin one."

third

Tom is standing on the third step.

throw

"Throw the ball, Tim," says Tom.

tight

"Hold on tight! Here we go."

tiny

Tim is looking at a tiny bug.
Can you see it?

together

The boys are swinging together.

top

Tom sleeps on the top.
Tim sleeps on the bottom.

train

Tim and Tom are running
their electric train.

tree

The boys are climbing a tree.

trip

Father is going on a trip
to another city.

---

truck

Tim has a dump truck.
Tom has a fire truck.

---

twins

Tim and Tom are twins.
Do they look alike?

Uncle Victor

umbrella

Uncle Victor opens his umbrella.

under

Now he is under it.

use

"I don't have to use
my umbrella anymore," says Uncle Victor.

vacation

Uncle Victor is enjoying his vacation.
"I don't have to work for two weeks."

valentine

Uncle Victor got a funny valentine

V
v

vegetables

How many vegetables can you name?

violin

Uncle Victor likes to play the violin.

visit

A friend came to visit Uncle Victor.

voice

The men are singing together.
They have good voices.

W

Walter and Wendy

wagon

Walter is giving Wendy a ride
in his wagon.

wait

"Wait in the car," says Father.
"I'll be back in a minute."

wake

"Wake up, Wendy.
It's time for breakfast."

walk

Walter and Wendy walk
to school together.

wall

Father is painting the wall.

want

"I have two plums. Do you want one?"

wash

"Wash your hands, Walter. Your face is dirty also."

watch

Father said, "My watch stopped."

water

"Come on in," says Walter.
"The water is just right."

wave

"Here comes a big wave!"

wear

"Wear your swimming cap, Wendy.
I'm wearing mine."

weather

"In hot weather this is the best way to cool off," says Father.

wet

"Don't get the blanket wet, Walter," says Mother.

whistle

The policeman blows his whistle.

win

"I think Wendy's going to win," says Walter.

wind

How strong the wind is!
See how it bends the tree branches.

window

"Who broke the window?" asked Father.
"I did," said Walter.

wing

Walter is painting the wings
of his airplane.

wish

"Make a wish, Wendy.
Maybe it will come true."

wood

Father put some wood on the fire.

woods

The family is walking in the woods.

X Y Z

xylophone

Wendy is playing her xylophone.

yard

The children and their baby cousin
are in the front yard.

X x Y y Z z

year

"Our cousin is one year old today," says Wendy.

young

"He is very young, isn't he?" says Walter.

zipper

"My zipper is stuck," says Walter.

ZOO

There are wild animals in this zoo.
Do you know their names?

rhinoceroses
elephants
X
x
Y
y
Z
z
alligators
tigers
lions
MONKEY HOUSE
monkeys

Words Used in This Book

This is an alphabetical list of all the words used in this book. It gives the number of the page for each word. Pictured words are in heavy black print.

This list can be used as a word finder. It can also be used to find out how many words a child can read without the help of pictures.

A

a, 6
able, 6
about, 6
above, 6
achoo, 87
across, 7
add, 7
address, 7
afraid, 7
after, 8
afternoon, 8
again, 8
against, 8
age, 9
ahead, 9
air, 9
airplane, 10
airplanes, 10
airport, 10
alike, 11
all, 11
alligators, 215
almost, 12
alone, 12
along, 12
alphabet, 12
also, 205
always, 103
am, 73
American, 70
among, 13
an, 13
and, 7
angry, 13
animal, 178
animals, 103
ankle, 27
another, 13
answer, 14
answers, 95
any, 180
anymore, 95
anyone, 168
anywhere, 115
apples, 76
April, 123
apron, 14
are, 11
arm, 27
around, 14
as, 12
asked, 126
asks, 23
asleep, 15
at, 28
ate, 61
August, 123
aunt, 138
automobile, 15
automobiles, 15
awake, 15
away, 16

B

baby, 18
back, 18
bad, 13
bag, 18
bakes, 105
ball, 18
balloon, 19
banana, 191
bananas, 76
band, 19
bank, 19
bark, 20
barks, 20
barn, 65
baseball, 20
basket, 20
bat, 20
bath, 20
bathroom, 158
be, 34
beans, 201
bears, 214
beat, 153
beautiful, 21
because, 88
bed, 139
bedroom, 21
bee, 72
been, 164
before, 38
begin, 21
begins, 112
begs, 28
behind, 22
bell, 22
belongs, 92
below, 22

C

D

desk, 50
desks, 50
did, 31
didn't, 68
different, 51
dig, 51
dime, 123
dinner, 51
dirt, 52
dirty, 41
dish, 97
do, 23
doctor, 52
does, 95
dog, 7
doll, 52
dollar, 123
dolls, 52
done, 60
don't, 34
door, 53
down, 53
dozen, 53
draw, 54
draws, 114
dream, 54
dreaming, 54
dress, 54
drew, 89
drink, 54
drinks, 29
drive, 55
drives, 55
drop, 55
drum, 19
dry, 55
ducks, 64
dump, 197

E

each, 39
ear, 27
early, 57
easy, 57
eat, 58
eats, 31
edge, 58
eggs, 53
eight, 132
elbow, 27
electric, 196
elephants, 215
eleven, 132
empty, 58
end, 59
engine, 59
enjoy, 59
enjoying, 200
enough, 60
ever, 60
every, 61
everyone, 141
everything, 61
eye, 27
eyes, 46

F

face, 63
fall, 167
family, 63
far, 121
farm, 64
farmer, 66
farmhouse, 64
farms, 46
fast, 66
fasten, 66
faster, 160
fat, 66
father, 67
February, 123
fed, 61
feed, 67
feeding, 140
feeds, 67
feel, 67
feet, 163
fell, 68
fence, 68
field, 64
fight, 68
fill, 69
filling, 144
find, 13
finger, 27
fingers, 179
fire, 69
first, 69
fish, 70
fit, 70
five, 132
fix, 70
flag, 70
flashlight, 70
flat, 71
float, 71
floor, 71
flower, 72
flowers, 84
fly, 72
food, 72
foot, 27
football, 30
for, 15
forget, 73
fork, 170
found, 73
four, 132
fourth, 73
fresh, 74
Friday, 49
friend, 74
friends, 148
friend's, 128
frighten, 75
frog, 173
from, 29
front, 75
frown, 179
fruit, 76
frying, 139
full, 58
fun, 77
funny, 63
fur, 67

G

game, 79
games, 79
garden, 79
gate, 79
gave, 40
get, 80
gets, 35
getting, 120
gift, 80
giraffes, 214
girl, 80
girls, 129
give, 81
gives, 81
giving, 20
glad, 81
glass, 81
glasses, 81
glove, 41
gloves, 82
go, 14
goat, 64
goes, 19
going, 16
gold, 82
goldfish, 144
good, 54
good-by, 82
goody, 51
got, 80
grade, 83
grandfather, 83
grandma, 83
grandmother, 83
grandpa, 79
grapefruit, 76
grapes, 76
grass, 83
gray, 44
great, 77
green, 44
ground, 84
grow, 84
growing, 79
guess, 84
gum, 84

H

had, 122
hair, 27
half, 86
half dollar, 123

hall, 86
Halloween, 86
hammer, 87
hand, 27
handkerchief, 87
hands, 41
hang, 87
hanger, 87
hangs, 128
happen, 88
happy, 88
hard, 180
has, 12
hat, 176
hate, 89
hats, 45
have, 60
having, 51
he, 8
head, 27
hear, 89
hears, 106
heart, 89
heavy, 90
heel, 27
hello, 90
help, 90
helping, 172
helps, 84
her, 50
here, 91
herself, 12
hide, 91
hiding, 20
high, 91
higher, 116
hill, 92
him, 26
himself, 86
hippopotamuses, 214
his, 92
hit, 92
hits, 87
hold, 93
holds, 93
hole, 93
home, 93
hop, 93
hope, 153
hops, 93
horn, 94
horse, 65
horseback, 156
horses, 155
hot, 94
house, 94
how, 12
hug, 104
hungry, 94
hunt, 95
hunts, 95
hurry, 95
hurt, 95

I

I, 19
ice, 97
ice cream, 97
if, 192
I'll, 90
I'm, 12
in, 8
Indian, 97
ink, 182
inside, 98
into, 9
invite, 98
iron, 99
irons, 99
is, 6
island, 99
isn't, 124
it, 7
its, 67
it's, 42

J

jacket, 101
January, 123
jar, 101
jet, 10
joke, 101
July, 123
jump, 101
June, 123
just, 126

K

kangaroos, 214
keep, 103
keeps, 26
kept, 72
key, 103
kick, 103
kind, 103
kindergarten, 104
kiss, 104
kitchen, 105
kite, 9
kitten, 144
knee, 27
knife, 105
knit, 105
knock, 106
knocks, 106
know, 106

L

ladder, 108
lamb, 65
lamp, 108
land, 108
large, 109
last, 109
late, 109
laugh, 110
laughing, 11
lazy, 110
leads, 141
leaf, 111
learn, 111
learned, 132
learning, 123
leave, 130
leaves, 111
left, 112
leg, 27
legs, 23
lemonade, 97
lemons, 76
let, 112
let's, 145
letter, 112
letters, 12
lettuce, 201
lick, 113
licks, 113
lies, 116
lift, 90
light, 113
lightning, 113
like, 113
limes, 76
line, 114
lions, 215
listen, 114
listening, 153
lit, 38
little, 66
live, 114
lives, 7
living, 158
log, 69
lollipop, 113
long, 115
longer, 185
look, 11
looking, 195
looks, 28
lost, 115
loud, 115
love, 116
loves, 116
low, 116
lunch, 116

M

made, 40
mail, 118
mailman, 138
make, 118
makes, 59
making, 126
mama, 172
man, 50
man's, 135

T

U

V

W

X

Y

Z

Book design by Willis Proudfoot
Color separations by American Litho Arts, Inc.
Printing by Von Hoffmann Press, Inc.